Wilderness Challenge

Written by Avelyn Davidson
Photography by Sarah Meghan Lee

U.S.A.

Meghan loves a challenge, so an Outward Bound trip to the Absaroka-Beartooth Wilderness in Montana sounds like an adventure not to be missed! Away from her home and family, Meghan has to depend on the group, and she learns how **teamwork** can help people survive in the wild.

teamwork working together

Contents

Wilderness Challenge

For Meghan, sneakers are out and hiking boots are in—at least, for the next two weeks. Meghan and five other young people, Chris, Josh, Anne, Harrison, and Pete, have joined an Outward Bound program designed to teach them about survival in mountain environments. For the next fifteen days, they will hike, camp, and rappel in the Absaroka-Beartooth Wilderness in the mountains of Montana.

"None of us had ever met before," said Meghan, "but it doesn't take long for you to get to know people when you are learning to depend on each other for survival."

rappel   to descend a cliff using ropes and a harness

Meghan soon discovered that nothing could beat the excitement of climbing a 50-foot rock face!

Bound for Adventure

The Outward Bound programs are designed to help young people push themselves to new heights, conquer fears, work as a team, and discover leadership qualities in themselves.

Another such program is the Spirit of Adventure in New Zealand, which teaches young people to crew a tall sailing ship. Each year, the program gives more than a thousand young people a taste of adventure on the high seas!

The Beartooth Mountains take their name from a sharp peak that resembles a bear's tooth. Eagles soar above the mountains, green meadows, and plateaus, which are home to animals such as deer, goats, wolves, and grizzly bears. "It's the most beautiful country I've ever seen in my life," said Pete from Maine.

Each day, Meghan and the others took turns navigating for the group. They learned to read a topographical map and choose the route to their next camp. They worked out the hazards they had to avoid and figured out the shortest route. "No one wants to carry those packs farther than they have to," Meghan said, laughing.

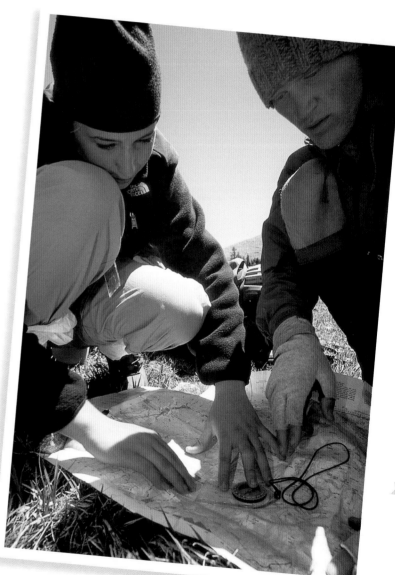

topographical showing the physical features of an area

Have you been camping in the wilderness? What was the greatest challenge you had to face?

Meghan and Josh examine a lightning mark on a tree. Thunderstorms occur frequently in this remote area, and lightning strikes are a common cause of wildfires.

7

Each day, the instructors pushed Meghan and the group a little harder and taught them more. The group learned survival techniques for the harsh wilderness environment, such as keeping warm, preparing food, and making shelters. At first, the high altitude made the young people feel tired and dizzy. Gradually, however, their bodies adjusted, and before long, the group was doing all the work and making decisions for themselves. "It wasn't easy," said Meghan. "We often felt like quitting. But after a while, we realized we could do it. We kept each other going and didn't give in."

"The magic of the scenery kept us going," said Josh. "You never knew what you might see around the next rock or over the next ridge."

Anne and Meghan link arms to cross a river safely. The more people there are linking arms in a line, the safer a river crossing is likely to be.

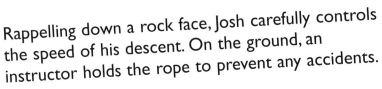

Rappelling down a rock face, Josh carefully controls the speed of his descent. On the ground, an instructor holds the rope to prevent any accidents.

The course instructor (right) shows his students exactly how to control a climbing rope from the ground. This is known as belaying.

This climbing exercise is all about trust. Blindfolded, Josh must trust his climbing partner on the ground to guide him to safe handholds and footholds.

Having learned to work as part of a team, Meghan and her friends now faced their biggest challenge—going solo! Alone, each member of the party hiked to an isolated spot and stayed there for two days and two nights. They were given food, as well as a sleeping bag and a tarpaulin for shelter. Chris from Minnesota thought it was the coolest thing he had ever done. "The stars at night are fantastic here," he said. "I lay awake trying to name the constellations." Harrison found the experience more difficult. "I learned that I relied on other people for company and entertainment."

Meghan finished the course feeling on top of the world. "I climbed to the top of a rocky pinnacle and watched the sun coming up. Now I feel I can go out and conquer the world!"

For Anne, the solo experience was a little scary. "The night noises were starting to get to me, so I stuffed tissues in my ears and pulled my sleeping bag over my head!"

Josh was fascinated by a porcupine that hung around his campsite. "I watched it for ages. I'd like to be a wildlife photographer."

Wilderness Safety Tips

- Tell someone exactly where you will be hiking and when you expect to return.
- Select a hiking route to suit your hiking ability.
- Check the weather forecast before setting out.
- Ask the park ranger if he or she is aware of any hazards along the hiking route.
- Carry an up-to-date map of the area and a compass.
- Hike in groups of four or more people.
- Take suitable warm, waterproof clothing.
- Wear comfortable hiking boots.
- Take a well-stocked first-aid kit.
- Take a flashlight with spare batteries.
- Carry matches in a waterproof container for emergencies.
- Carry enough food and water to last you the entire journey.
- Take a cell phone.
- Keep food safe from animals at night by putting it in a pack and hanging it from a tree.

Explore Wilderness U.S.A.

The United States is a country of great natural beauty and contrasts. When the first Europeans arrived in America, they found a land of ancient forests, high mountain ranges, and vast prairies covered with herds of buffalo. Most of those early settlers lived in rural areas and worked as farmers, trappers, fishermen, or lumberers.

Gradually, cities and towns grew in size and importance. Today, three-quarters of the population live in urban areas. However, Americans retain their love of the outdoors, and most cities provide parks where people can spend time away from the urban hustle and bustle. Some of these parks, such as Central Park in New York, have become home to large numbers of wildlife, such as raccoons, foxes, squirrels, and many species of birds.

Central Park, New York

Constitution Gardens is in Washington, D.C., the nation's capital. The park is on land that was originally beneath the Potomac River. The land was drained and turned into a park at the beginning of the 20th century.

On the Go!

How were the Grand Canyon's stripes formed?
Go to page 17

Which national park was the first in the world?
Go to page 18

Where is North America's highest mountain?
Go to page 23

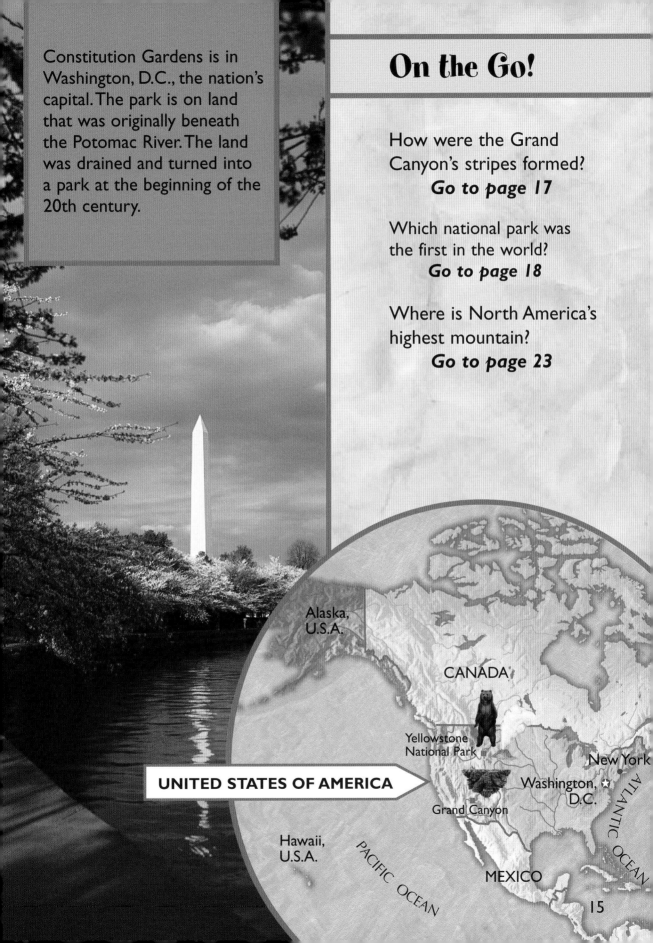

Alaska, U.S.A.

CANADA

Yellowstone National Park

New York

UNITED STATES OF AMERICA

Washington, D.C.

Grand Canyon

Hawaii, U.S.A.

PACIFIC OCEAN

ATLANTIC OCEAN

MEXICO

Natural Wonder

The Grand Canyon in Arizona is one of the natural wonders of the world. It is 277 miles long, one mile deep, and stretches 18 miles from rim to rim at its widest point. The canyon was formed over millions of years by water and wind erosion and the movement of the earth's plates. The Colorado River cut deep gorges in the rock, leaving candy-striped pinnacles and cliffs, and regular flash floods battered the canyon walls with rocks as large as trucks.

Today, the Glen Canyon Dam helps prevent flash floods from occurring. Even so, it is always best to check the weather conditions before hiking into the canyon.

The Grand Canyon is home to hundreds of animal species, such as the golden eagle.

erosion   the gradual wearing away of land by wind, water, or ice

Around four million people visit Grand Canyon National Park each year. The canyon's stripes were formed from colored sediments that were deposited long ago by the sea. Fossils of sea creatures can still be found at the Grand Canyon, even though it is now hundreds of miles from the coast.

National Parks

In 1872, the U.S. Congress created the world's first National Park, an area of natural beauty set aside "for the benefit and enjoyment of the people." Situated in the top left corner of Wyoming and spilling into Idaho and Montana, it was named Yellowstone National Park and quickly became famous for its hot springs, geysers, and other unusual features. Because of its protected status, it is one of the last places in the U.S. where animals live in nearly the same numbers and variety as before the coming of European settlers.

Today, the U.S. National Park System includes 54 national parks and hundreds of other unique areas of natural or historical interest.

Yellowstone's geysers and hot springs are caused by underground volcanic activity.

Yosemite Falls in Yosemite National Park, California, is America's highest waterfall. Yosemite is one of several national parks founded by the conservationist John Muir (1838–1914). Muir worked all his life to inform the public of the need to protect America's natural heritage.

Fire Watch

When forest fires broke out in Yellowstone National Park in July 1988, authorities at first let them burn. Fires are an essential part of many forest ecosystems, returning nutrients to the soil and clearing space for new growth. Some trees need the heat from fires to crack open their seed cases.

However, fires can also be destructive and deadly. In 1988, unusually dry conditions at Yellowstone caused the fires to rage out of control, eventually burning more than a third of the park's area. Today, park authorities take a cautious approach to forest fires. When human lives or property are threatened, the fires are quickly dealt with.

A fireman uses a special torch to burn off dry leaves and sticks on a forest floor. Fires lit for this purpose are called prescribed fires and can help prevent larger forest fires.

ecosystem   animals, plants, and their environment

Do you live near a forest or visit one regularly? If so, what can you do to help prevent forest fires?

Stopping Fire in Its Tracks

Airplanes and helicopters drop water or special chemicals on a fire to slow it down.

Firefighters clear wood and leaves from a strip in front of a fire to make a barrier called a firebreak. Backfires may be lit between the firebreak and the fire to burn off more dry material and make the firebreak area wider.

Fragile Frontier

Alaska, with its rugged scenery and often harsh climate, is sometimes called America's "last frontier." However, Alaska's landscape is fragile. This was shown in 1989, when an oil tanker called the *Exxon Valdez* struck a reef and spilled 11 million gallons of oil into Alaska's Prince William Sound, killing thousands of birds and mammals and polluting about 1,300 miles of coastline.

Pollution, drilling for oil, and mining are some of the many activities that can threaten wild places, such as Alaska. Although the U.S. has many laws to protect its wilderness areas, growing demand for natural resources is putting increased pressure on the environment. Conservation groups, such as the Sierra Club, work to prevent environmental damage before it occurs.

Workers remove oil-soaked sand from a beach in Katmai National Park, Alaska, after the *Exxon Valdez* disaster.

Mount McKinley, North America's highest mountain, is situated in Denali National Park in Alaska.

Did You Know?

Alaska has the largest reserves of oil in the United States, and the oil industry contributes billions of dollars each year to Alaska's economy. Drilling for oil is not allowed in the Arctic National Wildlife Refuge, a large protected wilderness area in the north of Alaska. Some people think parts of the refuge should be opened up for oil exploration. However, conservation groups argue that this would threaten many species that live in the region.

Do you think mining for oil and minerals should be allowed in wilderness areas?

The Trans-Alaska Pipeline carries oil from Prudhoe Bay in Alaska's north to the port of Valdez in the south.

What Do You Think?

1   Some teams work well together, and some teams don't. What are the secrets of good teamwork?

Teamwork is often part of our daily lives. What activities do you do as part of a team?

2   If you had to spend two days on your own, how do you think you would pass the time? What would you enjoy and not enjoy about the experience?

Index